Mind Power

The Never Revealed Secret Ways To Achieve Greatness Using Mind Mastery And Neuroplasticity

By John Waters

I0413042

Table of Contents

INTRODUCTION

Pop culture is inundated with characters who have powers of mind control and telepathy.

Emma Frost, a character in X-Men who is converted to the mutant side after the murder of her sister and brought to the mutant school to teach, has a telepathic affair with Jean Grey's husband. The affair culminates in Jean catching Frost and Cyclops in bed together in their minds and psychically humiliating Frost. Professor X, the founder of the mutant school, at one point has telepathic abilities that allow him to communicate with alien species all the way across the world and learn languages by tapping into the communication centers of their brains.

The Jedi in *Star Wars* have the ability to use the Force to cause people and objects to obey them. Using the mind control powers of the Force, Obi Wan is able to convince a storm trooper that, "These aren't the droids you're looking for."

Flotsam and Jetsam, the electric eels in *The Little Mermaid*, seem to hypnotize Ariel to get her to give in to her heart's desire and go to the sea witch, Ursula for help. A recent study by Vanderbilt University in Nashville reveals that eels not only have the power to zap their prey with 660 volts of electricity and paralyze them within 3 milliseconds, but they can project an electric current that can cause their prey to involuntarily twitch to give away its location. The makers of *The Little Mermaid* didn't know that eels had such powers, but apparently their characters did.

These characters and situations draw on powerful psychological questions: is the Biblical adage that people who lust after each other have already committed adultery in their hearts true scientifically? Can language be understood on a practical level by tapping into a certain section of the brain? Is it possible for people to harness electromagnetic power to use as their own? And finally, how do ethics fit into this picture?

Greatness

When the subject of human greatness arises, the age-old nature versus nurture argument often surfaces. Is one great because of the set of circumstances into which one is born, or is one great due to one's innate set of talents? Anecdotal evidence abounds to prove both cases, but I think that by proving both cases, we prove simply that nature and nurture both play pivotal roles in human greatness.

Greatness is defined by Miriam-Webster as being remarkable in magnitude, degree, or effectiveness; being markedly superior in character or quality; being eminent or distinguished; or being remarkably skilled (Greatness).

Shakespeare wrote in *Twelfth Night*, "Be not afraid of greatness: some are born great, some achieve greatness, and some have greatness thrust upon 'em'. Shakespeare seems to be onto something. Nature and nurture don't have to be mutually exclusive. After all, greatness is rarely comprised solely of talent. There's a mantra that rings through sports locker rooms that says, "Hard work beats talent when talent fails to work hard." On the other hand, hard work frequently doesn't seem to pay off in greatness, and, let's face it, some great people have little talent to speak of. So where's the balance, and how much control can we exert over finding the right combination of talent and circumstance?

Mastery

Mastery is more than mere proficiency or competency. Think Inigo Montoya in *The Princess Bride*. Inigo's mastery was obtained through years of practice and training. I had a teacher once tell me that if I wanted to be great at something, it wasn't enough to practice until I got it right; I had to practice until I couldn't get it wrong.

The science behind our ability to learn new functions and improve at or alter old functions is called neuroplasticity. Our brains have the ability to change with learning. While learning has always been an integral part of human history, the idea that the brain changes when we learn is relatively new to science.

For a long time, scientists thought that the brain was like a machine with sections corresponding to each function of the body. The phrase, "One function, one location," came into vogue in the 1860s after the surgeon, Paul Broca, dissected the brain of a stroke victim with no speech ability and found tissue damage in the left frontal lobe of the patient's brain. This was the tangible proof that the left frontal lobe was, indeed, associated with speech (Doidge, 2012). With this discovery came further research seemingly in line with the idea of the brain as a piece of machinery, with each section responsible for its own function of movement, perception, thought, or habit.

Later in the decade, a few studies emerged that indicated that the brain might be more than a complex piece of machinery. In 1868 Jules Cotard studied children with early massive brain disease in which the left frontal lobe was damaged, but the children could still speak. He found that another part of the brain took over the speech functions. Likewise, in 1876 Otto Soltmann studied dogs and rabbits with the motor cortex area associated with bodily movement removed and found that they could still walk. These experiments indicated that, while there are areas of the brain typically attributed to certain functions, these areas are not as rigid as scientists first thought. When damage occurs in certain areas, other areas of the brain can take over to perform those functions. This is an important discovery.

For a damaged brain, this means that recovery of damaged functions is possible. For an undamaged brain, this means that there are infinite learning possibilities available to you if you understand how your brain works and apply yourself. Nicholas Carr says, "The genius of our brain's construction is not that it contains a lot of hardwiring but that it doesn't". Unlike a computer, which is constrained both by its hardware and software, the human mind has an ability to learn and adapt with startling ease. For example, "Virtually any skill or talent can be created and perfected through training; people with no innate ability to remember numbers can memorize hundreds of decimals of pi through repeated training".

Through practice, you have the means of changing your brain's circuitry and transforming your life. "We all have some weak brain functions," says Doidge, "and such neuroplasticity-based techniques have great potential to help almost everyone. Our weak spots have a profound effect on our professional success, since most of our careers require the use of multiple brain functions". The purpose of this book is to give you an understanding of how your brain functions and provide you with the tricks you need to achieve your greatest self—whether that be your most creative, attractive, intelligent, intuitive, or athletic.

The following chapters and sections are ordered in a way that allows for maximum cohesiveness. The order is not meant as a series of cumulative steps but rather as a web of interdependent ideas.

CHAPTER ONE: SELF-AWARENESS

A distinguishing feature between people and the rest of the animal world is our propensity for self-awareness. We can use reason to weigh the pros and cons of performing a certain action. We can systematically perform the action. Then we can spend hours in post-decision dissonance fretting over whether we did the right thing. Animals, on the other hand, are limited by their instincts. It would be ridiculous to see a group of lions holding a discussion forum on whether it is morally right to eat zebras. Clearly, there is something different about humans.

The question of whether consciousness exists and whether we have it (and can a zombie logically exist?) has been around for thousands of years. Consciousness is a slippery concept and difficult to study, because if we have it then we must be using it to study it, which quickly becomes subjective and convoluted. One thing that seems pretty safe to note is that while the brain doesn't appear to have a centralized location that manages all other brain functions, the consciousness seems to be continuous and centralized.

Our conscious thoughts indicate that we don't act merely on instinct. According to Hanson and Mendius, "Only we humans worry about the future, regret the past, and blame ourselves for the present". Justification and rationalization form a large part of our conscious decision-making. We can list reasons why we should and shouldn't act in a certain way before and after we do it. We can act in ways that are contrary to our instincts and become convinced of things we are wrong about. We can identify when and why our instincts are wrong and brainstorm better and worse decisions for ourselves. We can develop self-control with the power to override our instincts.

Self-awareness can lead us to recognize the ways in which we can exert control in our lives and achieve greatness in whatever we pursue.

Synchrony

In 1965, Dr. Joe Kamiya was studying brain synchrony, which is when the brain's electrical activities are synchronized in one or more areas of itself. Previous studies had shown that synchronous activity most often happens when the brain is relaxed but alert. When synchrony is occurring, the brain performs better. Kamiya did an experiment to see if college students hooked to an EEG (a machine that measures brain waves) could learn to guess what state their brain was in. When he found that they eventually learned to accurately predict when their brains had entered the alpha state, he asked them to produce the alpha state on command. He found that they were able to learn to do that as well. Even more remarkable were the results of producing the alpha state for hours at a time.

Students reported feeling more relaxed, focused, and refreshed. Kamiya was not the first or the last to discover this.

At roughly the same time, in 1966, John Silva, a radio repairman, figured out a way of using self-hypnosis and concentrated relaxation to function at a more self-aware level on a daily basis. He hypothesized that tapping into alpha and theta brain waves while conscious would allow people to function at a happier, more creative level. When he tried this on himself, he found that it worked. He developed a series of techniques that he called the Silva Method. In a nutshell, he says that to bring yourself into the alpha and theta levels of consciousness, start by counting backward from a hundred, leaving two seconds between each number. Do this twice a day for ten days. For the next ten days, do the same thing, counting backward from fifty. For the next thirty days, decrease your count from fifty to twenty-five to ten to five. After fifty days, the idea is that you will be able to enter into the alpha state simply by counting backward from five. Participants in the Silva Method have reported greater focus and concentration, improved memory and attention to detail, and heightened senses.

A few years later, Dr. Les Fehmi found that the most efficient way of producing the alpha state in his subjects was to ask them to imagine the space between their eyes or their ears. This extended attention to space, or, as he would say, to nothing, he learned, was similar to meditation. By relieving the mind of its usual narrow focus, one can achieve greater focus on everything (Fehmi & Robbins, 2007).

Fehmi calls his method of obtaining synchrony Open-Focus. Mihaly Csikszentmihalyi calls it Flow. Buddhist monks call it meditation. The names and the techniques vary, but the concepts are the same. Spend some time every day not trying so hard; it will enable you to spend the rest of your time trying your hardest, and possibly even better.

Positivity

It is vital to note that negative experiences in our lives cling to us more easily than our positive experiences. Negativity is sticky, while positivity is smooth. The authors of *Buddha's Brain* urge readers to look at situations in terms of the positive. This sounds obvious, but it's harder than it sounds. The benefits of being self-aware are easy to bury under the drawbacks.

Hanson and Mendius suggest that to turn positive facts and positive experiences into stickier substances, you need to savor them and absorb the positive emotions associated with them. Live in the moment, and when good things happen to you, let yourself sink into the moment and fully feel that emotion. Take conscious note of the details. Perhaps all is not well in your life, but the sun is warm on your face or you're with someone you love. Even if it's a small moment, it is important. It is yours. By reinforcing this, you are rebuilding your neural circuitry toward a more positive outlook.

Instincts

Notice your gut reactions. Many studies have been done on thin-slicing, or the ability to look at a small segment of a personal interaction and make quick, accurate judgments about who the individuals are and how they will react in the future.

By analyzing a fifteen minute video segment of a couple talking about a conflict in their life, Professor John Gottman can predict with 95 percent accuracy which couples will stay together and which couples won't. He says that the biggest determining factor is the presence of contempt in their voices or faces.

Likewise, a doctor's likelihood of being sued can be seen by watching and listening to splices of their conversations with patients. Studies by Nalini Ambady show that the doctors most likely to be sued for malpractice aren't the least qualified. They aren't even the ones who make the most mistakes. They are the ones who spend less time with their patients, are less personable, and do less to make their patients feel taken care of emotionally. A few seconds is often all it takes to come to an accurate assessment of a doctor.

The same can be translated into ordinary life analyses. In basketball this is called court sense. In the military it's call coup d'oeil. Students who second guess themselves when choosing multiple choice answers on a test notice this when they change an answer only to discover that their original answer was correct.

While gut responses can be accurate in many situations, it's important to also recognize that sometimes gut feelings can result from unconscious prejudices. Thin-slicing can be accurate and necessary, but it is also the cause of subconscious racism. Outward displays of racism are socially unacceptable in most parts of the country, since the political successes of the civil rights movement; backlash against open displays of racism is seen in the news constantly. But inward, subconscious racism is harder to corral, because we don't always realize that it's there.

Becoming more self-aware is a steppingstone to recognizing and fixing your deficits on your way to your vision of greatness.

CHAPTER TWO: GENDER

Gender, Historically

More than 99 percent of male and female DNA is the same, but the less than 1 percent difference is incredibly important, both socially and scientifically. One study compared brain scans of men and women while they mentally rotated abstract, three-dimensional shapes. Researchers found that men and women demonstrated activation in different sections of the brain while they were problem solving, though they both were able to achieve the same results (Jordan, et. al., 2002). This study was enlightening, because it provided evidence that the differences in problem solving seen in men and women externally are present in the brain as well.

Men have a larger brain relative to their body size than women by 9 percent. In the past, this led people to believe that, besides reproductive capabilities, women were basically little men, inferior in intellect and reason. This "evidence" made it even easier to reinforce a patriarchal society.

In a test of gender bias, a group of researchers came up with a test called the Implicit Association Test, or IAT. In it, they timed participants while they put a list of words in either of two categories, "Male or career" and "Female or family." When they switched up the categories so that they read, "Male or family" and "Female or career," participants took a longer time completing the activity. They found that when biases exist, people unconsciously have a more difficult time doing things that require them to overcome these biases (Gladwell, 2005).

This experiment sheds light on the fact that despite decades of women's suffrage, our culture has still not subconsciously adjusted to women in stereotypically "masculine" career oriented tasks. Women have proved time and again that they have the same mental abilities.

Says Will Ferrel's character in *Anchorman*, "You're just a woman with a small brain. With a brain a third the size of us. It's science". It is science (sort of), but since the seventies, science has also discovered that smaller does not mean inferior. In fact, it's been repeatedly found that men and women have the same number of brain cells and the same mental capacities.

The bias still exists, despite the science, which is important to acknowledge as you set about achieving your goals.

Hormones and Society

Studies from the last decade show that biological differences between men and women derive almost entirely from differing hormone levels. Knowing these biological differences and which hormones are affecting your brain can help you set realistic expectations for yourself and form perceptions that are more true to reality.

Men and women have a lot of the same hormones, but in different quantities. For example, we all have estrogen, testosterone, vasopressin, oxytocin, and cortisol, but the varying quantities of each react together in different ways and cause the differences that drive our social realities.

For example, the oxytocin levels in a woman's brain cause her to think and behave in a more nurturing, selfless way. Men experience this hormone as well; it balances the more aggressive hormones like testosterone and Mullerian Inhibiting Substance (MIS) by lowering stress and blood pressure and making it easier to experience empathy and bond with their children.

Each of the hormones we experience cause certain behaviors and feelings, which account for the ways men and women act differently. While a fair argument can be made for socially conditioned behaviors, it's important to note the possibility that nature and nurture can react against each other in a cyclical manner.

Men are typically more aggressive, action-oriented, and competitive. As boys, they learn what it means to be a man from the important men in their lives; they stop crying when they hurt themselves, they participate in competitive contact sports, and they don't spend too much time thinking about feelings and emotions.

Women, on the other hand, typically relate to others on a more social level. Infant girls learn almost instantly to make eye contact with their mothers and others in their line of vision and react to facial expressions. According to Brizendine, by the time a girl is three months old, her skills with eye contact and facial gazing will have increased by 400%. She will grow up watching her mother and her society and draw cues from it that tell her that being a woman means being a mother and a nurturer and participating in quiet activities like dolly dress up and house.

Observation of children and adults and societal gender roles can easily lead us to believe that these roles are entirely socially constructed, but a long look at the developing brains of males and females reveals that there is biology behind gender norms that has been largely hidden until brain scan technologies emerged in recent decades.

In the early stages of pregnancy, the male brain is doused in high levels of testosterone, which kill off cells in the part of the brain used for communication skills and emphasize the cells for sex and aggression. Female brains don't experience this testosterone marinade in early formation. In fact, the communicating parts of the brain grow. When girls are born, they have a natural inclination for mutual gazing at their mothers and any faces that cross their vision, whereas a boy's attention is much more likely to be caught by moving objects. Studies show that from infancy, females are compelled to study faces, and this careful study teaches her to be sensitive to expressions and emotions. She learns to do things to elicit facial expressions and also learns subconsciously that an expressionless face is the result of her inadequacy (Brizendine, 2006).

Women's ability to read emotions increases into adulthood, and while it's first nature for most women to discern nuances in facial expressions and body language, it tends to be more difficult for men and develops much later.

So while the specific behaviors (playing dolls versus playing football) are learned behaviors, the hormones that drive our parents and siblings and peers to encourage these behaviors in each other appear to have a likely root in our biology.

Gender and Career

Extensive research has shown over and over that men and women are capable of achieving the same level of mastery in any subject, though, studies show, they frequently arrive at the same conclusions via different circuitry. The fact that there are fewer women in the math and science fields doesn't mean that they must be innately less intelligent when it comes to math and science. This has been the go-to assumption for centuries. Another assumption is that they are taught to prefer careers in language or the arts. This is undoubtedly true for some women; reasons for not choosing one livelihood for another are as numerous as people themselves. Neuroscience simply adds another layer.

It's likely, in many cases, that women tend to choose jobs and careers that allow them to be more social. The hormones in a woman's brain, and the well-developed communication circuitry frequently cause women who begin in the typically more solitary math and science fields to switch to something that allows them to interact more with other people at midlife (Brizendine, 2006).

Gender at Home

Sometimes it is painfully obvious that men and women experience emotions differently. What is less obvious is why that's the case.

One reason for emotional differences is because while male hormones are fairly stable throughout an adult man's life, a woman's hormones are in a constant state of flux. The sudden absence of the hormone allopregnenolone is responsible for causing irritableness or sadness right before a woman's period. In some women, anger and depression during PMS is extreme and can drastically alter a woman's experience of reality such that she feels hopeless. Brizendine says that,"[I]f in the name of free will—and political correctness—we try to deny the influence of biology on the brain, we begin fighting our own nature. If we acknowledge that our biology is influenced by other factors, including our sex hormones and their flux, we can prevent it from creating a fixed reality by which we are ruled".

Another reason for emotional differences is due to differing usages of two simultaneously operating emotional systems called the mirror-neuron system (MNS) and the temporal-parietal junction (TPJ). The MNS causes you to mirror another person's emotional state in our brains—in other words, you feel empathy. The TPJ separates yourself from the other person, which helps you look at a problem or situation more objectively.

Women, when listening to another person speak, will use the MNS through the entire interaction. Men will briefly feel the pain of empathy from the MNS and then switch over to trying to solve the problem with the TPJ. The TPJ prevents a person's thought processes from being infected by the other speaker's emotions, which strengthens the ability to understand the situation and get at a solution (Brizendine, 2010). This is why he's trying to solve her problem, and she thinks he hasn't empathized with her and doesn't care.

It seems like an overgeneralization to say that men are the problem solvers and women are the relaters, and it is. Due to different hormonal levels at birth and throughout our lives, our brains might be predisposed to function via different circuit routes (hundreds of years of anecdotal and scientific evidence can back this up), but the vast plasticity of the human brain leaves little doubt that a man is as different from a woman as he is from every other man.

Whether you are a man or a woman will not predispose you for greatness, but understanding sex and gender from a neuroscientific perspective as well as understanding the integral role they will always play in your life is important. "Biology powerfully affects but does not lock in our reality. We can alter that reality and use our intelligence and determination both to celebrate and, when necessary, to change the effects of sex hormones on brain structure, behavior, reality, creativity—and destiny," Brizendine says.

CHAPTER THREE: HABITS

We are what we repeatedly do. Our habits form a huge part of our daily life. Understanding what habits are, how they form, and how to change them is key to mastery and greatness in any skill. Talking about habits is like playing a game of Good News, Bad News.

The bad news is, we don't make as many choices every day as we'd like to believe we do. Many of the things that we assume are choices are actually a series of habits that we've "hardwired" into our brains over time. "Most of the things we know exist outside of our conscious awareness," Richard Restak says (2006). Philosopher Michael Polanyi called this tacit knowledge. Neuroscientists call it the cognitive unconscious. The good news is, without giving up some of the control of conscious decision-making, our brains would be continuously mired in the work of breathing, moving feet, eating, and performing any number of other boring daily rituals.

The basal ganglia is a region of the brain thought to be responsible for cuing habitual behaviors. Through an experiment monitoring brain activity in rats running through a maze, scientists at MIT determined that once the rats had run the maze many times, they not only got faster at navigating, but their brain activity levels decreased. In other words, once they knew the maze, the rats relied on autopilot to get them to the reward at the end of the maze (Duhigg, 2012).

Professor Larry Squire used this method on Eugene Pauly, a victim of viral encephalitis, a disease that damaged the part of his brain that forms new memories, by creating a memory game and drilling him on it. He found that, though Eugene could not explain how he knew which cards were correct or which house was his or how to get to the kitchen, his basal ganglia stored these habits and guided him outside of his conscious recognition.

This is an important discovery, because it shows that once a habit is learned, the brain no longer needs to be involved in active decision-making. You can and do perform many of your daily activities without actively thinking them through.

Map, Not Machine

Brain circuitry, rather than being like machinery, is more like a complicated topography or map. In a road system, if a bridge goes out on the main road, we reroute. Through repeated rerouting, or using different circuitry, the brain discovers the fastest possible way to get to the original destination. The more we have to deal with our problems in a new way, the faster and more efficient we become.

A great example of brain remapping can be found in the experience of Cheryl Schlitz, a victim of the antibiotic gentamicin. After prolonged use of gentamicin, due to negligent doctors, Cheryl suffered severe damage to her vestibular apparatus, which made her feel like she was perpetually falling. The vestibular apparatus controls balance. Without it, she constantly wobbled in all directions and had to focus all of her energy on staying upright. As a result, she was constantly fatigued and suffered a plethora of new anxieties and fears about herself and her future. As a last ditch effort, she went to see Paul Bach-y-Rita, a researcher in brain plasticity, who had invented a way to retrain the brain to balance via an ordinary-looking helmet and an electrode covered tongue piece. The helmet and tongue piece together acted as a substitute vestibular apparatus.

When Cheryl tilted forward, the electrodes on the front of her tongue created a bubbling sensation. When she tilted backward, the electrodes at the back of her tongue bubbled. After a few training sessions with this device, it was discovered that her brain relearned how to balance, and she experienced increasing residual effects from wearing the device. After many months, she no longer needed to wear the hat and tongue piece at all, because her brain had remapped her vestibular apparatus in another location and practiced the learned new circuits until the change was permanent (Doidge, 2007).

Doidge records another example of brain plasticity in Barbara Arrowsmith Young, who learned to overcome severe learning disabilities by addressing them head-on. She was born with an asymmetrical brain incapable of spatial reasoning, which caused her to hurt herself running into things. Even worse, was her extreme difficulty with understanding the relationships between symbols. She couldn't understand math, grammar, or logic, but she had an excellent memory and learned to get through school by rote memorization. She could not read clocks or social cues and understood nothing in real time. She had to spend much of her time reviewing past events to understand what had happened.

When she was accepted into graduate school, she started seeking solutions to her learning problems. She tried doing things to compensate for her deficiencies, but she had so many that she decided a program of compensation would have been too time consuming. Through discovery of papers by Luria and Rosenzweig, who described her experience and, in the case of the latter, provided hope that the brain might be capable of overcoming such disabilities, she realized that she must attack her problem head on—by exercising her weakest functions. With flash cards and tireless repetition, she taught herself to recognize and interpret hands on a clock. This breakthrough led her to attack and vanquish her other disabilities and to eventually open a school for children who might benefit from the curriculum she'd designed for herself.

Learning New Tricks

The good news is, loads of studies from the past few decades show that you can, indeed, teach an old dog new tricks.

Some of our best studies on habit formation come from advertising. Claude Hopkins, one of the single most influential people in advertising (he was famous for making Schlitz beer, Palmolive soap, Quaker Oats, Goodyear tires, and Van Camp's pork and beans famous), shared his rules of marketing through habit formation in conferences later in his career. He said that two things were necessary: one must find an obvious cue, and one must clearly define the reward.

What he didn't realize explicitly at the time was that the cue and reward system could not work when the people most in need of forming the new habit did not recognize the cue. For example, if a person who smells terrible doesn't realize that he smells bad, he won't seek the reward of smelling good by using perfume or bath soap. Also, nagging doesn't work; compliance that is forced will ultimately fail.

Thus, a cue and a reward aren't enough to make a certain activity into a habit. "Only when your brain starts expecting the reward…will it become automatic" (Duhigg, 2012). This expectation can also be called a craving. Just like a smoker craves nicotine and reaches for a cigarette, so can a runner learn to crave the endorphins or that certain sense of accomplishment from doing a healthy activity.

If you want to form a new habit, you need to come up with a reward for yourself that will facilitate a craving, whether that's the idea of your new bikini body or that work promotion or the satisfaction of checking a task off a list. Then you need to give yourself a cue. For example, put your running shoes on immediately after getting off work to remind you that you must run. Anticipate the reward that you have in place for yourself, like the endorphins, the satisfaction of finishing well or an hour of guilt-free TV. Every time you run, do these things. Once you've developed a craving for your reward, you will find that you can't go without your habit.

Here is another example of the cue and reward system: When you get up in the morning, you have morning breath. That's the cue that reminds you to brush your teeth. The minty, tingling feeling of your mouth after you brush is your reward. Your mouth feels fresh. Toothpaste doesn't have to be minty and tingly to do its job, but the sensation makes us believe that it's working and inspires us to keep up the habit.

Changing Bad Tricks

The bad news is, you can't extinguish a bad habit. The good news is that by understanding the Golden Rule of habit change, you can replace the bad habit with a good habit. As you now know, cravings are what fuel habits. These cravings are obsessions that drive your behavior. A person with a smoking habit will crave nicotine. Prolonged restraint increases the craving, until the person finds that their hand automatically reaches for a cigarette to satisfy the craving.

But you don't want to crave nicotine anymore. So, using the same cue and the same reward, you must create a new routine. When you find yourself craving nicotine, figure out a new activity that can easily replace bringing a cigarette to your mouth. Maybe you grab a piece of minty gum. Maybe it's hard candy.

Perhaps one of the most successful examples of a habit change program is Alcoholics Anonymous. At first glance, the twelve steps seem like a strange conglomeration of arbitrary activities and spirituality. On second glance, we see that the Golden Rule of habit change is very much present. Step four encourages one to take inventory of one's faults, or, in other words, evaluate the cue, routine, reward cycle. Step five requires admitting the faults to another person.

Since the cues of many alcoholics don't derive from a desire to be drunk, but rather a desire to forget or to relieve loneliness, being part of the AA group gives the participant a social community with which to form different routines. A member who correctly identifies what her cue is can much more effectively change her habit, and the community is there to support her.

Nathan Azrin, one of the developers of habit reversal training said, "It seems ridiculously simple, but once you're aware of how your habit works, once you recognize the cues and rewards, you're halfway to changing it" (Duhigg, 2012).

If you are trying to revamp multiple habits in your life, identify a "keystone habit" to change, and you will be able to systematically reprogram the other routines in your life. According to Duhigg, "There is nothing you can't do if you get the habits right."

CHAPTER FOUR: BODY AND PHYSICAL HEALTH

Your body is in your head, Chopra and Tanzi argue. A lot of research supports this. Several brain health studies done on mice showed that mice on low fat diets experienced better memory and fewer plaques than mice on high fat diets. Furthermore, mice who exercised experienced even greater memory and brain health, even if they stayed on a high fat diet (Carmona, 2014). In other words, a healthy diet is good for your brain, but exercising is even better.

When it comes to weight loss, the odds are not in your favor. According to Aamodt and Wang, the brain is not naturally inclined to help you lose weight. Metabolism, leptin, insulin, and your hormones all conspire to adjust your body's fat storage to keep you at your present weight and body mass index. In fact, the neurons in charge of promoting food intake inhibit the neurons responsible for reducing food intake, but the reverse is not also true. This is why it is so much easier to gain weight than it is to lose it.

"Your brain will always be working toward its own automatically set goals, so any changes you make to your eating and exercise habits will also need to be permanent to remain effective" Aamodt and Wang also say. Thus, it's important to make dietary changes that you can realistically follow for the rest of your life. Fad diets typically don't work long term because they are not sustainable. Can you imagine eating cabbage for the rest of your life? Yuck. What a lot of diet programs miss is that your body needs a certain number of calories per day in order to maintain optimal body and brain functioning. Likewise, certain levels of nutrients contribute to your overall good health.

In order to create good habits of healthy eating or retrain bad habits, use the cue and reward system to create a craving. Once you have a craving for eating your veggies, your body will help you perpetuate the great, new you.

Perhaps more effective than careful dieting is exercise. While eating right is important, exercise will do the most for you when it comes to losing and maintaining weight as well as overall brain health. A 2011 study from the University of Arizona found that "physically fit older men and women showed fewer age-related changes in their brains" and that the more fit they were, the fewer signs of age they showed (Carmona, 2014). Keeping your body behaving like it's young is a matter of learning to treat it like it's young, it would seem.

Exercise boosts the metabolism by twenty to thirty percent. Muscle at rest burns more calories than fat at rest. Belly fat is particularly dangerous, because it sends dangerous hormonal signals to the rest of the body. Converting fat to muscle through repeated exercise increases metabolism.

Aerobic exercise is the most important for brain health, studies show. Examples of this are walking, running, biking, swimming, dancing, or anything that causes an elevated heart rate for a prolonged period of time. The downside to many of these activities is that they allow your mind to wander. Playing sports that require speed, absolute attention, and cognitive flexibility like tennis will enhance your brain function even more (Carmona, 2014).

Dr. Costas Karageorghis at Brunel University in England found that listening to music that is between 120 and 140 beats per minute can maximize an aerobic workout (Karageorghis & Priest, 2008). If you really like music, consider using music as a reward in your cue and reward cycle to kill two birds with one metaphorical stone.

Sleep and stress levels can play a disconcertingly large role in the overall health of your body. Regular sleep deprivation and stress cause a decrease in metabolism that makes it difficult to lose weight and extra easy to gain it.

Get yourself on a realistic sleep schedule. Figure out if you are on a less than 24 hour circadian rhythm (morning person) or a more than 24 hour circadian rhythm (night person) and adjust your sleep schedule to optimize your sleep habits. Not every person is the same. Some people need more than eight hours of sleep at night, some people feel sluggish if they get more than six or seven. Familiarize yourself with your body's natural sleep patterns.

Stress releases corticotropin, a hormone that makes it difficult to lose weight. Too much stress can almost make us "forget" how to make changes to reduce that stress, limiting the mental flexibility needed to find alternative solutions and triggering general adaptation syndrome (GAS), better known as burnout, which makes us feel unmotivated and mentally exhausted (SharpBrain). Basically, being perpetually stressed out causes you to eventually forget how to take care of yourself.

Fortunately, there are also ways to train your brain to deal with stress. Find what triggers your stress. If a bad habit is causing it, retrain your habit. If it's constant busyness, learn how to tap into some alpha waves.

Graceful Aging

Cells are constantly changing. Cells that stop changing die. People are similar, but on a much larger level. "The most crippling aspects of aging tend to involve inertia" (Chopra & Tanzi, 2012). Habits built early in life are easier to sustain in old age. The reverse is also true; habits not built earlier in life are harder to attain. It's difficult to build on what you don't have.

Chopra and Tanzi say that the key to setting yourself up for graceful aging is creating a matrix for better choices. This goes back to the idea of the cue and reward system. Cupboards with no junk food could be part of such a matrix, but be careful not to strip your life of pleasures such that your matrix is discouraging. Discouragement causes a lot of failure.

Another part of your matrix could be to surround yourself with people who have good lifestyles. The habits of others are contagious. Spend time with people who eat well and care for their bodies, and you will feel encouraged to do likewise. Also, "success comes when people act together; failure tends to happen alone" (Chopra & Tanzi, 2012).

By creating a matrix centered around people who are important to you, activities that you like, and food that is nutritious and pleasurable, you increase your chances of continued health when one of these things inevitably is altered or disappears. For example, the passing of your spouse could be devastating if your spouse is your only strong social connection. However, if you have a group of friends or family to help you through when you're down, you are much more likely to pull through the trauma.

Beware of junk foods. There is a difference between knowing what's good for you and acting on it, and snacking is a huge opportunity to either give your body a healthy fruit boost or bring it down with starchy, fatty snacks. The snack food industry has a term called the "munch rhythm" that describes eating snack foods on autopilot. Once you've made certain flavors a craving, you will eat them without realizing what you're doing. This is dangerous for all people, but it is especially damaging the older you get, when potato chips mean more to your body than a little bit of bloating.

In terms of medical health and wellbeing, people don't die of old age. Death happens when a key body system breaks down, bringing the rest of the body with it. You can't escape death, but by keeping your body's key systems healthy, you can fight off death while maintaining a strong, healthy life.

Taking care of your body leads to a better brain. In return, a healthier brain helps you take care of your body.

CHAPTER FIVE: MEMORY

As you get older, your brain gets rid of synapses that aren't used and strengthens the connections that are used. Experience determines which connections will be strengthened and which will be pruned; active connections will remain while those that no longer receive or give signals die out (this happens through a process called apoptosis). This is called synaptic pruning. Literally, you need to use it or you'll lose it.

Today memory is seen differently than it has throughout history. Before text-based media and the printing press there was a rich oral story-telling tradition in which knowledge was passed from the old to the young through stories and traditions. Intelligence and knowledge were memory.

Even after written language was invented, the oral tradition persisted. The Socratic method of learning consisted of a student asking questions of a teacher, and the teacher asking questions in return to spur a student's learning. Jesus used verbal story-telling to educate his followers and pass on wisdom.

The sound of spoken language to a listener, like puns and assonance were important: "It is not the healthy who need a doctor but the sick."

In the 18th and 19th centuries, classical education focused on memorizing long poems in foreign languages and "fanatical attention to handwriting." Memorizing long poems improved auditory memory, and practicing handwriting, particularly cursive, strengthened one's speed and fluency of speaking and reading. A lot of attention was given to "exact elocution." These skills have since been dismissed as pointless. Children are not taught cursive when word processing is far more pervasive, and they are not taught to memorize long poems and lists of facts when it's so easy to look things up online. In removing the emphasis on memory and handwriting from modern curriculum, students lose the valuable tools that came as a result of the time spent learning these skills.

The Lincoln Douglass debates are a great example of classical education at its finest. The speakers could give long speeches without using notes. They could speak eloquently in front of large groups with minimal preparation. Today, Powerpoint presentations are used as the ultimate compensation for a weak premotor cortex (Doidge, 2007), because people are not trained from childhood to speak extemporaneously anymore. The good news is, it's possible to learn.

Remember Barbara Arrowsmith Young, the woman who trained her brain to overcome her symbolic recognition disabilities? In the school she founded, she trained children with weak auditory memories by having them listen to CDs and memorize poetry. She helped strengthen children's visual memories by having them trace letters of Persian and Urdu (Doidge, 2007). Many of the students who graduated from Barbara's school had mastered their weaknesses to the extent that these new skills were superior to the average person's.

Creative Memory

According to 8 time world memory champion, Dominic O'Brien, memory is intertwined with creativity. He says that making unconventional associations that draw on small details and each of the senses is key to creating memorizations that will stick. He offers lists of words and encourages the reader to spend several minutes dwelling on detailed associations with each word—kitten, rainbow, toy, birthday, ice cream, snow, church, cushion, sand, toe nail. Vivid associations allow one to draw links between words, that, in turn, help one create memories.

Memory is not a fixed entity; it's very open to suggestion. Elizabeth Loftus, a researcher and collector of false memories says that it's common for people to genuinely believe that a story they heard sometime actually happened to them. She says that what we're doing when we're relating a memory is constructing, not recollecting. This means that when she suggests a vivid account of a person getting lost in the mall as a child, she can get up to fifty percent of participants to believe that it happened to them (George, 2013). This has had implications in the courtroom with people getting others convicted on the basis of repressed memories—memories, Loftus says, that are more likely constructions based on powerful suggestion.

What does this have to do with memorizing a list of objects? Well, it's simple: when you form detailed constructions of each item on the list, you are more likely to remember the item. Even further, when you imagine each item on the list in relation to the next item, it makes it easier to remember. This is different from a false memory, but it builds on the same concept; creating mental images helps you recall the words or numbers you've associate with them.

O'Brien used a method that he calls the journey method. In it, he associates familiar places and objects in order with the items he is memorizing. In 1933, German psychologist Hedwig Von Restorff was able to conclude that "the strongest criteria for recall is individuality" (O'Brien, 2011). If he's trying to memorize a sequence of fifty-two cards, he'll choose a location with a natural sequential order— walking down the street in his hometown, for example. He'll assign an object, person, or animal to each card. Once he's learned which card is which object (For example, say the 5 of clubs represents his dog), he can imagine the journey of walking through town and attributing each individual card with the next place on his route.

To memorize a long list, like the order of all the cards in a shuffled deck, practice the journey method. Don't expect to be fast at it at first, but the more you do it, the faster you will become.

Repetition retrains brain circuitry more effectively than anything else. Hebb's rule says that, "Cells that fire together wire together." The more you repeat something, the more defined the brain's neural circuits become, and the easier it gets for you to perform the action with less conscious effort. This applies to memorizing a poem, learning an instrument or language, or memorizing the correct series of movements to hit a baseball. It's called building muscle memory.

Other Memory Tips

Exercise is another great way to enhance memory, especially doing aerobic activities like dance and tennis that require absolute attention and cognitive flexibility.

Read critically. Of course you should read for pleasure, but also challenge yourself with higher reading levels or approach your pleasure reading from a more critical standpoint. Try thinking through the plot structure or characterization of the novel you are reading or try reading adult nonfiction that isn't from the self improvement section of the library or bookstore. If you are interested in the environment, find environmental research studies to read. Academic studies can be difficult to read, but the more you read them, the easier time you will have understanding them. In turn, you will find that the more you think critically about your reading, the easier time you will have remembering it and drawing connections to it in other parts of your life.

Don't think too hard when learning something new. Paying too much conscious attention while learning a new task can cause our brains to think less accurately and efficiently. Restak advises that you let your brain learn at its own pace. He cites an experiment done by psychiatrist Paul Fletcher on volunteers tasked with pressing buttons to correspond with highlighted boxes on a computer screen. He found that the participants performed best when they relaxed and didn't think too hard. When they were told that the highlighted boxes were patterned and instructed to learn the pattern, they performed with far less accuracy and speed (Restak, 2006).

Eliminate distractions while you are trying to learn something. Say the thing you wish to memorize out loud. Make an acronym. There are hundreds of tips you can find on memorizing. They all come down to being creative. Your memory is bound by your own creativity.

CHAPTER SIX: CREATIVITY

Creativity encompasses nearly everything we do, whether it is art or science or daily tasks. Even our memories are entwined in our creativity. All of us are, in one way or another, creative. We tend to think of creativity in conjunction with the arts, which is not wrong, but to stop with art and music would be selling ourselves short. "Creative IQ is the ability to incorporate new ideas into established ways of doing things, leading to a change in viewpoint," Carmona says (2014).

Albert Einstein said, "After a certain high level of technical skill is achieved, science and art tend to coalesce in esthetics, plasticity, and form. The greatest scientists are always artists as well."

Historically, painters and sculptors like Leonardo da Vinci, Michelangelo, Donatello, Raphael, and other Renaissance artists were both artists and mathematicians. Leon Battista

Alberti, in his book called *On Painting*, emphasized how important it was for a painter in the fifteenth century to have a thorough understanding of geometry. He said that a painter could never be great without knowing the relationships between shapes and lines. The Renaissance Man was one who was a master of all trades, and judging by their masterpieces, there's little to dispute with that claim. Beyond being objects of beauty and cultural relevance, paintings of the Renaissance era formed public opinion. Caravaggio painted a known prostitute as the virgin in *The Death of the Virgin*, which didn't go over well, if you can imagine that. Masaccio painted two oblivious dandies wearing the rich textiles of the Brancacci family business in the middle of a fresco of Saint Peter's *Raising of Tabitha* and *The Healing of the Cripple* to make fun of the wealthy Brancacci family who commissioned the work.

Many of today's most promising artists and creative minds go into advertising.

Advertising companies have done some of the most groundbreaking studies on habit formation in existence, which have revolutionized selling techniques. Procter and Gamble employed scores of researchers, analysts, and artists to dream up the perfect campaign for Febreze. When targeting consumers with bad smells in their homes didn't work, they went back to the drawing board and came up with a new idea; what if instead being a scentless odor remover, they gave it a distinct scent and marketed it as the final step to a clean room? They went to town on this new idea and the result was huge profits for Proctor and Gamble and bonuses all around.

To become a more creative, successful problem solver, take advantage of both your talent and your external resources. Embrace those alpha waves. "When one has greater scope and immersion of attention, creative problem solving in every context—social, academic, professional, and athletic—is facilitated," say Fehmi and Robbins (2007).

Nurture your nature by giving yourself time and space to daydream. Albert Einstein said, "Creativity is the residue of time wasted." You can bet he's not talking about the sort of time wasting that happens when one sits passively in front of a TV show. "Most jobs and many leisure activities—especially those involving the passive consumption of mass media—are not designed to make us happy and strong. Their purpose is to make money for someone else. If we allow them to, they can suck out the marrow of our lives, leaving only feeble husks," says the author of *Flow* (Csikszentmihalyi, 1990). Take breaks from your work to let your mind wander or to actively engage in something else, but resist giving your mind passively to mass media.

Nature your nurture by finding other creatively minded people and places that nurture your creativity. Shakespeare found Elizabethan London when theater was booming. The Italian

Renaissance greats found Florence. C.S. Lewis found the Inklings.

Another creative pointer is to ask hard questions and look for meaningful answers. This is a less obvious piece of advice than it sounds. Fear of offending people has had a way of squelching questions and obscuring answers in the last couple of decades. The gospel of tolerance is more like the gospel of eggshells. But ask yourself, would movies like *The Matrix* and *Inception* be quite the same if Descartes hadn't asked if he existed?

Seek answers in fields of knowledge that are unfamiliar to you. Once you've mastered one field, you've formed a solid foundation for mastering another. Paul Erdos, a prolific Hungarian mathematician of the twentieth century, was never okay with letting himself get bored, and thus was constantly dabbling in different fields (Lehrer, 2012). The more you learn about different bodies of knowledge, the more you will realize that they are all connected.

There is no math *or* art; there is only math and art and a perception of the two being mutually exclusive.

Motivation

"For artists, scientists, inventors, schoolchildren, and the rest of us, intrinsic motivation—the drive to do something because it is interesting, challenging, and absorbing—is essential for high levels of creativity," Pink says (2009). This is why rewards sometimes don't work. Once you've passed a threshold, incentives can have an opposite effect, because they can eliminate intrinsic motivation. With no intrinsic motivation, work that once might have been pleasurable is now simply work.

Be careful about the kind of reward you assign yourself in your habit creation when it comes to creativity, because contingent rewards typically will eventually strip creativity of intrinsic motivation. "Mass leisure, mass culture, and even high culture when only attended to passively and for extrinsic reasons—such as the wish to flaunt one's status—are parasites of the mind. They absorb psychic energy without providing substantive strength in return. They leave us more exhausted, more disheartened than before" (Csikszentmihalyi, 1990).

Intrinsic motivation is important for a couple of reasons. First of all, motivation derived from the pleasure of the activity is a lot harder to take away from you. Even if extrinsic motivators like monetary reimbursement are taken away, you still have the pleasure of the work. Second of all, artists with intrinsic motivation to produce art have more successful careers than artists who are more extrinsically motivated. Ironically, the intrinsically motivated painters and sculptors who care less about the world's affirmation are the ones most likely to eventually receive it (Pink, 2009).

CHAPTER SEVEN: TECHNOLOGY

Our technology has created a world in which behaviors and habits can be predicted with disconcerting accuracy. Advertisers and politicians can use brain imaging research to get us to buy the latest gadget or vote for a certain up and coming politician. As studies in neuroscience extend from academic and medical settings to personal and social settings, neuroscience will have the opportunity to both inform and invade our lives.

A technique called memory morphing is used in advertising to describe when marketers transpose one image over another to persuade consumers to believe in a memory that didn't happen. A study by Braun, Ellis, and Loftus found that by using autobiographical advertising, marketers can cause people viewing their ads to increase their belief in a memory that they did not have. Participants in the study viewed a Disney ad asking them to remember shaking hands as a child with an impossible character like Ariel or Bugs Bunny. They reported with greater certainty that they had shaken hands with these characters as a child at Disneyland after viewing the ad. It was found that "autobiographically focused advertising can make events, even impossible ones (Bugs Bunny isn't a Disney character, and Ariel wasn't a character at any of the Disney resorts during participants' childhood) seem more likely to have happened to consumers as children.

Similarly, studies have shown that not only are memories suggestible, but so are political affiliations. Participants in studies viewing photos of political candidates whose faces had been morphed with percentages of their own faces revealed that the participants were more likely to respond favorably to the candidate in the altered photo than to the original. With databases of drivers' license photos along with other demographic information becoming more and more accessible, what happens if it's discovered that morphing small percentages of an individual's face with a political candidate can manipulate election results (Restak, 2006)?

Is it okay for marketers to knowingly alter peoples' memories to persuade them to buy a product? Is it okay for politicians to use our faces to manipulate our vote? It seems that people should at least be informed that these kinds of manipulation are possible.

The Dark Side

Brain plasticity is awesome because it allows us to constantly learn new things and adapt to our surroundings. Brain plasticity can also be harmful, because our surroundings do not always have our best interests in mind.

Take the internet, for example. The internet allows us to have a seemingly infinite store of organized information right at our fingertips. It enables us to shop, pay bills, mail things, and plug into our jobs without ever leaving our desks. This sounds convenient, but is it? Says Nicholas Carr, author of *The Shallows: What the Internet Is Doing to Our Brains*, "When we go online, we enter an environment that promotes cursory reading, hurried and distracted thinking, and superficial learning". With everything at our fingertips, we live in a perpetual information overload. We never have time to sink into a great article. If it takes longer than a minute or two to scan, well, email calls. "The internet delivers precisely the kind of sensory and cognitive stimuli—repetitive, intensive, interactive, addictive—that have been shown to result in strong and rapid alterations in brain circuits and functions," Carr says.

If the alpha state has a polar opposite, surely it's the internet. In meditation, one empties one's brain and lets oneself think about nothing. In surfing the web, one opens one's mind to everything until one finds oneself clicking mindlessly between windows and browsers.

The president of a job search counseling company said, "Do you really want to enjoy your summer vacation? Then keep your cell phone handy and stay on top of those emails." To enjoy our vacation, we need to keep up with work while we are on vacation? That's counter-intuitive. Yet, with company down-sizing happening all the time, and with the advancement of devices that keep us in the loop—whether we want to be or not—it's dangerous to really check out. Having the means to work any time, any place affects the way we react to the space around us. We lose the ability to compartmentalize. Vacation isn't so much a vacation as it is a shift from working in the office to working on the beach or in a hotel room. We are trained to believe that learning to multi-task is a valuable skill when in reality it is merely "learning to be skillful at a superficial level" (Carr, 2011). In our age of information, we have the ability to know less, because more is a few clicks away.

Nigel from *The Devil Wears Prada* says, "Let me know when your whole life goes up in smoke. Means it's time for a promotion." Our brains are wired to associate our self worth with our jobs and vice versa. For a person whose identity becomes the job, the consequences of losing that job can be devastating.

Consequences

An increase in machine-automated prompts that replace people like on the phone and at the airport, make face-to-face interactions a lot less frequent. The fMRI scans of the brain show that the neural passages used for making small talk with a secretary or ticket agent are completely different from those used for pressing buttons on a phone to speak with a different department or communicating with an airport check-in machine. Desire for efficiency and economy is decreasing face-to-face time, which is having an impact on our ability to empathize with others (Restak, 2006).

Over-exposure to tragic news events halfway around the world triggers emotional burnout. Between December of 2004 and October of 2005, when natural disasters were reported on in vivid detail and in rapid succession, peoples' monetary donations waned along with their compassion and attention. This burnout, in many cases, becomes associated with anxiety and depression. As world events over which we have little or no control are increasingly available within minutes of happening, it is important to remind ourselves to place things in appropriate perspective. Compassion for fellow humans on the other side of the globe is important but shouldn't come at the expense of those who deserve compassion in our own communities and shouldn't come at the expense of our mental health. Letting ourselves get dragged down is of no use to anyone.

In the future, fMRI brain scans might be able to show things happening in the brain that contradict a person's present behavior. For instance, insurance agencies and job interviewers might be allowed to look at these scans as predictors of future behavior, thus giving them scientific evidence in favor of greater discrimination than is already possible. A man whose fMRI scan shows that he's susceptible to violent behavior might be denied a job even if he's never displayed violent behavior in the workplace, and even if he never does in the future. Neuroscientists say that the scans do not provide absolute data and must be taken with caution.

The medium is the message, media ecologist Marshall McLuhan says. The media we use shapes the way our minds think. Recognizing this is key to deciding what we will allow to influence our brains. The internet, hyperlinks, smart phones, and e-readers have caused us to expect constant stimulation and distraction. We don't write in a notebook with a number two pencil anymore. We tap on the touch screen of our tablet, which also has the capacity to play movies, games, surf the web, chat with our friends, and give minute by minute updates on anything we can think of.

Children are growing up more bored than ever before by life outside of a computer game and prone to behavior and attention deficit problems. We are losing the ability to concentrate on one thing for a prolonged period of time, because we have conditioned our fingers and our brains to flip quickly between multiple screens. We tell ourselves that we are maximizing our efficiency by multi-tasking when we're actually inhibiting ourselves from sinking into deep intellectual concepts and thinking through our problems with the focused energy of generations before us.

As a culture, we are experiencing a decrease in memory because we are no longer forced to memorize things like spatial directions and countries; it's easy to use a GPS or look them up online. We are confident in our ignorance.

We've put our brains into our technology and left them there.

Being self-aware enough to realize these pitfalls can help you to use technology with caution. Your smart phone is not innately harmful to you, but the way you use it can be, and the way you let it use you, can be. Understanding the ways in which the things and the people around you can impact your brain is what gives you the freedom to choose your influences, and, in turn, the ability to master your mind.

CONCLUSION

On Paradoxes

The human mind is full of paradoxes. I like a room to be cold when I'm sleeping, but I refuse to turn on the air conditioning in the summer. My vegetarian friend staunchly believes that killing animals is morally wrong and that meat is unhealthy, but she won't give up bacon. My brother was having a hard time meeting eligible women in his day-to-day life and turned to online dating, but there he found so many choices that he got overwhelmed and gave up on meeting people online. These are trivial examples, but let's extend the paradox to something that's not.

The cell phone was invented so that we can stay connected to each other even when we are not together. When the idea of carrying a cell phone first started gaining traction, it was a tool available in case of an emergency or unexpected change of plans (and for workaholics). As phones became smaller and shinier, the idea caught on. Parents started giving them to their teenagers when they passed their driving tests so that they could keep better tabs. It became a way to touch base, as well as something of a security blanket. Don't leave home without your phone; how will I know if something happens to you?

Then, the cell phone industry produced a series of revolutions that changed the way we use a phone. Text messaging made asynchronous phone communication possible. We can communicate with people even in situations that are not friendly or conducive to talking on the phone. We don't want to intrude on someone with a phone call, so we send them text messages that constantly intrude but "not in real time" (Turkle, 2011). The ability to check email and go online from a cell phone opened even more venues for communication and convenience. Today, one can essentially have an entire home office on their cell phone. Smart phones have made it possible to do everything from navigate the city to check into flights, all while texting, emailing, snap chatting, and playing a game of *Clash of Clans*. It's uncommon to see someone simply walk down a street or wait at a bus stop without taking out their phone to check their email or send a quick text or—heaven help us— look at this morning's weather forecast. Our phones connect us, almost literally, to everyone and everything in the world, while concurrently distracting us from the present. We never take mental breaks anymore. Even waiting in line at the grocery store we have a hard time just standing there letting our minds wander.

It's become easy to use our phones as mediators of everything. For example, I'm about to quote some pithy statements from Sherrie Turkle's *Alone Together*, a book which resides on the book shelf next to my couch about six feet from where I'm sitting. Yet, I just caught myself typing it into my search engine on my phone. Is this because I believe that my phone will be more efficient at finding the exact quote I'm looking for? Nope. It's a habit. I'm responding to a cue (wanting to look something up) by following a routine (a quick internet search on my phone) in order to obtain a reward (the satisfaction of finding the answer I'm looking for).

The great paradox of phones is that while they connect us to the world, they inhibit our connection this moment with these people in this space. It used to be that our biggest distractions at dinner were our own minds. Now we can't go out on a date anymore without bringing our entire social network. "We enjoy continual connection but rarely have each other's full attention," Turkle says (2011).

On Being in the Moment

Being in the moment is hard. I can blame it on my phone or laptop or a culture that has re-formed my brain circuitry to have an addiction to constant sensory stimulation. But at the end of the day, I am the one responsible for my own level of self-awareness.

It's hard, because even when I'm doing something I genuinely like to do, I find myself looking forward to when I've completed the activity. I go out with friends, and even when I'm having a genuinely enjoyable time, I catch myself wishing to be alone in my bedroom replaying the evening's events in my head instead of living them right now. I take a walk in the woods, and as my eyes rest on a turning maple, I am struck by the thought that this tree looks remarkably like the picture of the tree hanging above my desk, but perhaps that one was straighter and a little more golden.

Maybe you recognize these things in yourself too, and they catch you off guard. Why do you look forward to the memory of the moment before the moment itself has passed? Is this because social media has subconsciously convinced you that the point of doing anything fun is so that you have pictures to post of it online later? It's a joke that's not quite funny, like your left hemisphere hasn't quite kicked in yet.

At this point, you've read this book, and you've maybe tried some of the suggestions in it. If so, you've realized that this isn't a quick fix plan to make you instantly look and feel fantastic while reciting entire movies after one viewing. Perhaps you've heard the saying that anything worth doing isn't going to be easy. The brain is complex. Changing its patterns takes time and patience and repetition. Mastery takes all of these things and an awareness of perceived versus actual limitations. Sometimes you are like a horse tethered in place by a folding chair; it is not the chair and chain that keep you from moving but your perception of yourself in relation to the chair and chain.

You *can* do it, and though you'd like to become a master overnight, remember that the process is the story, and every master has a story.

BIBLIOGRAPHY

Aamodt, S., & Wang, S. (2008). *Welcome to your brain: Why you lose your car keys but never forget how to drive and other puzzles of everyday life*. New York: Bloomsbury.

Alberti, L. (1991). *On Painting*. New York: Penguin Classics.

Andreasen, N. (2006). *The creative brain: The science of genius*. New York: Plume.

Begley, S. (2007). *Train your mind, change your brain: How a new science reveals our extraordinary potential to transform ourselves*. New York: Ballantine Books.

Blackmore, S. (2005). *Consciousness: A very short introduction*. Oxford: Oxford University Press.

Braun, K., Ellis, R., & Loftus, E. (2002). Make my memory: How advertising can change our memories of the past. *Psychology and Marketing, 19*(1), 1-23. Retrieved April 12, 2015, from http://faculty.washington.edu/eloftus/Art icles/BraunPsychMarket02.pdf

Brien, D. (2011). *You can have an amazing memory: Learn life-changing techniques and tips from the memory maestro.* London: Watkins Pub.

Brizendine, L. (2006). *The female brain.* New York: Morgan Road Books.

Brizendine, L. (2010). *The male brain.* New York: Three Rivers Press.

Carmona, R. (2014). *Canyon Ranch 30 days to a better brain: A groundbreaking program for improving your memory, concentration, mood, and overall well-being.* New York: Atria Books.

Carr, N. (2011). *The shallows: What the Internet is doing to our brains.* New York: W.W. Norton.

Carter, R., & Frith, C. (1998). *Mapping the mind.* Berkeley, CA: University of California Press.

Chopra, D., & Tanzi, R. (2012). *Super brain: Unleashing the explosive power of your mind to maximize health, happiness, and spiritual well-being.* New York: Harmony Books.

Csikszentmihalyi, M. (1991). *Flow: The psychology of optimal experience.* New York: Harper Perennial.

The devil wears Prada [Motion picture]. (2006). 20th Century Fox Home Entertainment.

Doidge, N. (2007). *The brain that changes itself: Stories of personal triumph from the frontiers of brain science.* New York: Viking.

Duhigg, C. (2012). *The power of habit: Why we do what we do in life and business.* New York: Random House.

Fehmi, L., & Robbins, J. (2007). *The open-focus brain: Harnessing the power of attention to heal mind and body*. Boston: Trumpeter Books.

George, A. (2013, September 8). I Could Have Sworn...An interview with false-memory expert Elizabeth Loftus. *New Scientist*.

Gladwell, M. (2005). *Blink: The power of thinking without thinking*. New York: Little, Brown and Company.

Greatness [Def. 3, 5, 9, 10]. (n.d.). *Merriam-Webster Online*. In Merriam-Webster. Retrieved April 11, 2015, from http://www.merriam-webster.com/dictionary/greatness.

Hanson, R., & Mendius, R. (2009). *Buddha's brain the practical neuroscience of happiness, love, & wisdom*. Oakland, CA: New Harbinger Publications.

Is Self-Awareness Humanity's Greatest Trait? (2014, February 25). *Knowing Neurons*.

Jordan, K., Wüstenberg, T., Heinze, H., Peters, M., & Jäncke, L. (2002). Women and men exhibit different cortical activation patterns during mental rotation tasks. *Neuropsychologia, 40*(13), 2397-2408. Retrieved April 12, 2015, from http://www.ncbi.nlm.nih.gov/pubmed/12417468

Karageorghis, C., & Priest, D. (2008). Music in Sport and Exercise : An Update on Research and Applicatio. *The Sport Journal*. Retrieved April 10, 2015, from http://thesportjournal.org/article/music-sport-and-exercise-update-research-and-application/

Lehrer, J. (2012). *Imagine: How creativity works*. New York: Houghton Mifflin Harcourt.

News.com.au. (2014, December 5). Electric Eels Have Mind Control Powers. *New York Post*.

Pink, D. (2009). *Drive: The surprising truth about what motivates us*. New York: Riverhead Books.

Restak, R. (2006). *The naked brain: How the emerging neurosociety is changing how we live, work, and love*. New York: Harmony Books.

Schwartz, J., & Begley, S. (2002). *The mind and the brain: Neuroplasticity and the power of mental force*. New York: Regan Books/HarperCollins.

Silva, J., & Miele, P. (1977). *The Silva Mind Control Method*. New York: Simon and Schuster.

Six tips to build resilience and prevent brain-damaging stress. (2013, May 20). *SharpBrains*.

Turkle, S. (2011). *Alone Together: Why We Expect More from Technology and Less from Each Other*. New York: Basic Books.